CHRISTMAS
WITH
Mary & Martha

Dishin' Up Desserts & Hope

BARBOUR
PUBLISHING

Published by Barbour Publishing, Inc., P.O. Box 719, Uhrichsville, Ohio 44683, www.barbourbooks.com

Our mission is to publish and distribute inspirational products offering exceptional value and biblical encouragement to the masses.

Member of the
Evangelical Christian
Publishers Association

Printed in Canada.

5 4 3 2 1

CONTENTS

And she shall bring forth a son, and thou shalt call his name JESUS:
for he shall save his people from their sins.
MATTHEW 1:21 KJV

Meet Mary & Martha. . .

If you love baking up treats at Christmastime and savoring the sweet aromas coming from your kitchen, then this holiday cookbook is just for you. Featuring everything from festive cookies and candies to cakes and pies—if it'll sweeten up your seasonal celebration, it's in here!

We'll be appearing throughout the book, offering you tips and inspiration to make your Christmas just a bit merrier—*and* more meaningful.

Ready to dish up some desserts and hope this season? Roll up your sleeves, put on that apron, and. . .

Happy cooking!

With love (from our kitchen to yours),
Mary & Martha

Holiday Cookies & Bars

...That, of course, is the message of Christmas. We are never alone.
Not when the night is darkest, the wind coldest, the world seemingly most indifferent.
For this is still the time God chooses.

TAYLOR CALDWELL

Angel Cookies

1 cup sugar
1 cup butter or margarine, softened
1 egg
1 teaspoon vanilla
½ teaspoon almond extract
2 cups flour
½ teaspoon baking soda
½ teaspoon cream of tartar
¼ teaspoon salt
Water
Sugar

Beat together sugar and butter at medium speed until creamy. Add egg, vanilla, and almond extract, beating well. Reduce speed and add flour, baking soda, cream of tartar, and salt. Shape dough into 1-inch balls. Dip top of each ball into water, then into sugar. Place the balls on an ungreased cookie sheet, 2 inches apart.
Bake at 375° for 7 to 9 minutes. Makes about 3 dozen cookies.

Soft cookies are better for mailing than crisp ones.

Bon-Bon Christmas Cookies

4 ounces cream cheese, softened
½ cup butter-flavored shortening
2 cups flour, sifted
Water
1½ cups powdered sugar, sifted
2 (10 ounce) jars stemless maraschino cherries, drained

In medium bowl, stir together cream cheese and shortening until well blended. Stir in flour, using your hands, if needed, to help form dough. If mixture seems too dry, add 1 to 2 teaspoons water. Cover and chill several hours or overnight. Preheat oven to 375°. Lightly grease cookie sheets. Before rolling out dough, dust rolling surface heavily with powdered sugar. Roll out dough to ⅛-inch thickness. Cut into 1 x 4-inch strips. Place cherry on end of each strip. Roll up each strip starting with cherry. Place on prepared cookie sheets and dust with powdered sugar. Bake for 7 to 10 minutes in preheated oven. Cookies should brown slightly. After baking, dust again with powdered sugar. Allow cookies to cool before serving, as cherries are very hot!

Candy Cane Twists

1½ cups powdered sugar
1¼ cups butter or margarine, softened
1 egg
1 teaspoon peppermint extract
1 teaspoon vanilla
2¾ cups flour
¼ teaspoon salt
⅓ cup candy canes or peppermint candy, finely crushed
¼ teaspoon red food coloring

Beat together powdered sugar, butter, egg, peppermint extract, and vanilla at medium speed until creamy. Reduce speed and add flour and salt. Divide dough in half. Stir candy into one half of dough and beat food coloring into other half. For each cookie, roll 1 teaspoon of each dough into 4-inch-long rope. Place ropes beside each other and twist them together. Place on ungreased cookie sheet and curve one end of cookie to make candy cane shape.
Bake at 350° for 10 to 12 minutes. Makes about 4½ dozen cookies.

Chocolate Crinkles

1 cup cocoa
2 cups sugar
2 teaspoons vanilla
½ teaspoon salt
½ cup vegetable oil
4 eggs
2 cups flour
2 teaspoons baking powder
Powdered sugar

Combine first eight ingredients, mixing well. Refrigerate overnight. Form balls and roll in powdered sugar. Bake at 350° for 10 to 12 minutes. Sprinkle with powdered sugar after baking if desired.

Dear Lord, help me to keep my eyes fixed on You throughout the Christmas season. When the commercialism of the holiday threatens to snuff out the real meaning of Christmas in my heart, remind me of the gift of Hope You sent on that silent night so long ago. Amen.

O little town of Bethlehem,
how still we see thee lie!
Above thy deep and dreamless sleep
the silent stars go by.
Yet in thy dark streets shineth
the everlasting Light;
The hopes and fears of all the years
are met in thee tonight.
PHILLIPS BROOKS

Cinnamon Blossoms

1 cup butter or margarine, softened
¾ cup sugar
1 egg yolk
1 teaspoon vanilla
2 cups flour
1½ teaspoons cinnamon
¼ teaspoon salt
60 mini chocolate kisses

Combine butter, sugar, egg yolk, and vanilla, beating on medium speed until creamy. Reduce speed and add flour, cinnamon, and salt. Fill cookie press with dough. Press dough onto ungreased cookie sheet, placing cookies 1 inch apart. Bake at 375° for 8 to 11 minutes. As soon as cookies are removed from oven, place 1 chocolate in center of each. Makes 5 dozen cookies.

Cottage Cheese Cookies

Though they sound a bit unusual, these are melt-in-your-mouth delicious!

1 cup small-curd cottage cheese
2 teaspoons butter, softened
2 cups flour
3 tablespoons butter, melted
¾ cup brown sugar
¾ cup walnuts, chopped

Blend together cottage cheese and butter, then add flour. Roll out into ⅛-inch-thick circle on floured board. Spread with melted butter. Sprinkle with brown sugar and walnuts. Cut pie-style, then roll from large to small end of wedge like a croissant. Bake at 400° for 10 minutes. Store in sealed tin in refrigerator.

Lemon Butter Cookies

2 cups unsalted butter, softened
1 cup sugar
6 egg yolks
1 tablespoon vanilla
2 drops yellow food coloring
Zest of 2 lemons
5 cups flour
1 egg

Cream together butter and sugar. Add egg yolks, vanilla, food coloring, and lemon zest; mix well. Gradually add flour while stirring. Chill for 1 hour. Roll out to ¼-inch thickness and cut in shapes desired. Beat remaining egg; brush each cookie with beaten egg. Place on parchment-lined cookie sheet. Bake at 325° for 24 minutes or until lightly golden.

Norwegian Cookies

COOKIES:

1⅓ cups sugar
1 cup butter or margarine,
   softened
2 eggs
1 teaspoon vanilla
3 cups flour

1 teaspoon baking powder
2 cups (12 ounces) semisweet
   chocolate chips
3 tablespoons sugar
¾ teaspoon cinnamon

Mix together sugar and butter at medium speed until creamy. Beat in eggs and vanilla.
Reduce speed and add flour and baking powder. Stir in chocolate chips by hand. Divide
dough in half on lightly floured surface. Divide each half into thirds and shape each third
into 10-inch roll. Place on ungreased cookie sheets, two rolls per sheet, at least 2 inches
apart. Flatten each roll with moistened fork to about ½-inch thickness. In separate bowl,
combine sugar and cinnamon for a topping. On each roll, sprinkle about ½ teaspoon
topping mixture. Bake at 350° for 13 to 15 minutes. Slice diagonally into 1-inch
strips while still warm. Makes about 6 dozen cookies.

Oatmeal Chocolate Chip Cookies

2½ cups oats
1 cup butter, softened
1 cup brown sugar
1 cup sugar
2 eggs
1 teaspoon vanilla
2 cups flour

½ teaspoon salt
1 teaspoon baking soda
1 teaspoon baking powder
2 cups (12 ounces) chocolate chips
1 (4 ounce) chocolate bar, grated
1½ cups walnuts, chopped

Put oats in blender or food processor; blend to a fine powder, then set aside. Cream butter with sugars until fluffy. Add eggs and vanilla; mix together with blended oats, flour, salt, baking soda, and baking powder. Stir in chocolate chips, chocolate bar, and nuts. Roll into balls and place 2 inches apart on lightly greased cookie sheet. Bake at 375° for 10 minutes.

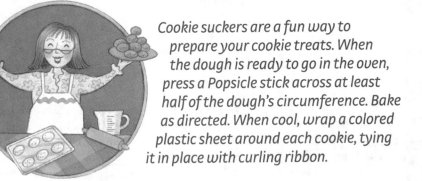

Cookie suckers are a fun way to prepare your cookie treats. When the dough is ready to go in the oven, press a Popsicle stick across at least half of the dough's circumference. Bake as directed. When cool, wrap a colored plastic sheet around each cookie, tying it in place with curling ribbon.

Orange Shortbread Fingers

¾ cup flour
3 tablespoons cornstarch
¼ cup sugar
Zest of 1 orange
¼ teaspoon salt
7 tablespoons unsalted butter, cut up
2 tablespoons sugar

Preheat oven to 300°. Grease 8 x 8-inch baking pan. Into medium bowl, sift flour and cornstarch. Add ¼ cup sugar, orange zest, and salt. Using fingertips, work butter into dry ingredients until mixture resembles fine crumbs. Knead mixture until it forms a dough, then press it into prepared pan. Score dough into 24 narrow rectangles and prick with tines of fork. Sprinkle with 2 tablespoons sugar. Bake for 30 minutes or until a pale golden color. Remove from oven and leave shortbread to cool in pan until it holds its shape enough to turn out onto a rack. When completely cooled, cut shortbread into fingers along scored lines. Cookies can be stored in airtight container for up to one week. Makes 24 cookies.

Peanut Butter Chocolate Kiss Cookies

½ cup shortening
¾ cup peanut butter
⅓ cup sugar
⅓ cup brown sugar, packed
1 egg
2 tablespoons milk

1 teaspoon vanilla
1⅓ cups flour
1 teaspoon baking soda
½ teaspoon salt
Sugar
1 cup (6 ounces) chocolate kisses

Cream shortening and peanut butter. Add sugars, egg, milk, and vanilla. Beat well. In large mixing bowl, combine flour, baking soda, and salt. Gradually add creamed mixture to flour mixture and blend thoroughly. Shape dough into 1-inch balls; roll in sugar. Place on ungreased cookie sheet. Bake at 375° for 10 to 12 minutes. Remove from oven immediately and place unwrapped kiss on top of each cookie. Remove from cookie sheet and cool.

Red Ribbons

Red ribbons add color and beauty to a cookie assortment.

1 cup butter, softened
2½ cups flour
½ cup sugar
1 egg, slightly beaten

1 teaspoon vanilla
¼ teaspoon salt
Strawberry jam or raspberry jelly

Beat butter with electric mixer on medium to high speed for 30 seconds. Add about half of flour, then sugar, egg, vanilla, and salt. Beat until thoroughly mixed. Add remaining flour, mixing until dough sticks together to form a ball. Lightly knead ball. Divide cookie dough into 8 equal portions. On lightly floured surface, roll each portion of dough into 9-inch rope. Place ropes on ungreased cookie sheet about 2 inches apart. Press groove down length of each rope with handle of wooden spoon. Bake at 375° for 10 minutes. Spoon jam or jelly into groove and return to oven, baking until edges begin to brown slightly (about 5 minutes). Cool on cookie sheet for 5 minutes. Using large spatula, remove cookies to cutting board. Drizzle glaze over hot cookies. Cut into 1-inch slices. Move cookies to wire rack to finish cooling.

GLAZE:

Water   ¾ cup powdered sugar

In small bowl, mix enough water with powdered sugar to form a glaze.

Snowflakes

1 cup butter-flavored shortening
1 (3 ounce) package cream cheese, softened
1 cup sugar
1 egg yolk
1 teaspoon vanilla
1 teaspoon orange zest
2½ cups flour
½ teaspoon salt
¼ teaspoon cinnamon

Preheat oven to 350°. In medium bowl, cream together shortening, cream cheese, and sugar. Beat in egg yolk, vanilla, and orange zest. Continue creaming until light and fluffy. Gradually stir in flour, salt, and cinnamon. Fill cookie press and form cookies on ungreased cookie sheet. Bake in preheated oven for 10 to 12 minutes. Remove from cookie sheet and cool on wire racks.

Spend some time sharing your hopes and dreams for the coming year with your family. Then dedicate one evening each week during which you gather together to pray and ask the Lord's blessing on your family in the new year.

"If you believe, you will receive whatever you ask for in prayer."
MATTHEW 21:22

Snowman Butter Cookies

1 cup butter, softened
½ cup sugar
¼ teaspoon almond extract
2½ cups flour
1 teaspoon water
Red and green food coloring
Black and orange jimmies or sprinkles

Cream butter, sugar, and extract. Gradually beat in flour and water. Place ⅓ cup mixture in small bowl and tint red. Place another ⅓ cup mixture in small bowl and tint green. Set both aside. Shape remaining dough into twelve 1-inch balls and twelve 1½-inch balls. Place one smaller ball above one larger ball on ungreased baking sheet; flatten slightly. Use 2 teaspoons colored dough and form into hat (make six of each color). Place above head. Make scarf by forming ¼ teaspoon each color into 3-inch rope. Twist ropes together, leaving one end a little "unraveled." Place scarf around snowman's neck. Insert jimmies or sprinkles for eyes and nose. Bake at 350° for 15 to 18 minutes or until set. Cool on baking sheets. Makes 12 snowmen.

Super Chocolate Icebox Cookies

1¼ pounds bittersweet chocolate,
  chopped
¾ cup unsalted butter
1⅓ cups sugar

4 large eggs
1 tablespoon vanilla
¾ cup flour
1½ cups semisweet chocolate chips

Line 8 x 8-inch baking pan with double layer of plastic wrap or waxed paper. Melt chocolate and butter in heavy saucepan, stirring constantly until smooth. Cool slightly. Whisk in sugar, then eggs and vanilla. Stir in flour. Stir in chocolate chips. Pour dough into prepared pan and smooth evenly. Cover with plastic and refrigerate overnight. Remove from pan and cut dough into 3 even bars (about 2½ x 8 inches each). (If making ahead, wrap in plastic and place in freezer bag. Thaw in refrigerator overnight before continuing.) Line cookie sheets with baking parchment or Exopat liners. Slice into ½-inch-thick slices and space about 2 inches apart on cookie sheet. Bake at 350° for approximately 15 minutes, or until puffed in center and wrinkled on top. Store in airtight container.

*This cookie dough works
 well to refrigerate or freeze
 and bake as needed.*

Surprise Packages

1 cup butter, softened
1 cup sugar
½ cup brown sugar
2 eggs
1 teaspoon vanilla
3 cups flour
1 teaspoon baking soda
¼ teaspoon salt
48 thin-layered chocolate mint wafers

Cream butter and sugars until light and fluffy. Beat in eggs and vanilla. In separate bowl, combine flour, baking soda, and salt. Gradually add to creamed mixture. Mix well. Divide dough in half; wrap each in plastic wrap and refrigerate for 1 to 2 hours. Preheat oven to 375°. Work with half the dough at a time. Using 1 scant tablespoon dough, cover each mint, forming rectangular cookie. Bake for 10 to 12 minutes. Cool. Can be decorated with icing to look like wrapped packages. Makes 4 dozen cookies.

Thumbprints

½ cup unsalted butter, softened
½ cup peanut butter
1¼ cups sugar
1 egg
2 tablespoons milk
2 cups flour
⅔ cup raspberry jam

Using electric mixer, beat together butter and peanut butter. Add sugar and beat until fluffy; then beat in egg and milk. Add flour, stirring with spoon until thick dough forms. Place in small, covered bowl and refrigerate at least 2 hours or until well chilled. Preheat oven to 350°. Roll dough into 1-inch balls and place 2 inches apart on buttered cookie sheet. Gently flatten balls with palm of hand and make small indentation in each with thumb. Fill each indentation with ½ teaspoon jam. Bake for 13 to 15 minutes or until edges are lightly browned.

Almond Bars

BASE:
1 cup flour
2 tablespoons powdered sugar
½ cup butter, softened

Combine all base ingredients, mixing well. Press dough into 9 x 9-inch baking pan.
Bake at 350° for 15 minutes.

TOPPING:
4 tablespoons butter
½ cup brown sugar
1 teaspoon vanilla
¼ cup cream
1 cup almonds, sliced

In double boiler, boil butter, sugar, vanilla, and cream for 3 minutes. Remove from boiler
and stir in almonds. Spoon almond mixture over base. Bake 15 minutes longer.

Butterscotch Bars

CRUMB MIXTURE:

2 cups (12 ounces)
  butterscotch morsels
½ cup butter or margarine

2 cups graham cracker crumbs
1 cup walnuts, finely chopped

Preheat oven to 350°. Grease 9 x 13-inch baking pan; set aside. In medium saucepan, melt morsels and butter over low heat, stirring often. Remove from heat. Stir in crumbs and nuts. Press half of crumb mixture into bottom of pan. Pour filling over crumb mixture in pan. Sprinkle remaining crumb mixture on top. Bake for 25 to 30 minutes or until toothpick inserted in center comes out clean. Cool completely on wire rack. Refrigerate.

FILLING:

1 (8 ounce) package cream
  cheese, softened
1 (14 ounce) can sweetened
  condensed milk

1 egg
1 teaspoon vanilla

In large mixing bowl, with electric mixer on medium speed, beat cream cheese until fluffy. Beat in sweetened condensed milk, egg, and vanilla until smooth.

Chocolate Cappuccino Brownies

BROWNIE LAYER:

1 tablespoon instant espresso powder
½ tablespoon boiling water
4 ounces fine-quality bittersweet (not sweetened) chocolate, chopped
6 tablespoons unsalted butter, cut up
¾ cup sugar
1 teaspoon vanilla
2 large eggs
½ cup flour
¼ teaspoon salt
½ cup walnuts, chopped

Preheat oven to 350° and butter and flour 8 x 8-inch baking pan, tapping out excess flour. Set aside. Dissolve espresso powder in boiling water. In heavy 1½-quart saucepan, combine chocolate and butter with espresso mixture; melt ingredients over low heat, stirring until smooth; remove pan from heat. Cool mixture to lukewarm, then whisk

(cont.)

in sugar and vanilla. Add eggs one at a time, whisking well until mixture is glossy and smooth. Stir in flour and salt until just combined; stir in walnuts. Spread batter evenly in pan and bake in middle of oven for 22 to 25 minutes or until tester comes out with crumbs adhering to it. Cool brownie layer completely in pan on rack. Spread frosting evenly over cooled brownie layer. Chill frosted brownies for 1 hour or until frosting is firm. Spread glaze carefully over frosting. Chill brownies, covered, until cold, at least 3 hours. Cut chilled brownies into 24 squares and remove them from pan while still cold. Serve brownies cold or at room temperature. Brownies keep, covered and chilled, for 5 days. Makes 24 brownies.

CREAM CHEESE FROSTING:
4 ounces cream cheese, softened
3 tablespoons unsalted butter, softened
¾ cup powdered sugar, sifted
½ teaspoon vanilla
½ teaspoon cinnamon

In bowl with electric mixer, beat cream cheese and butter until light and fluffy. Add powdered sugar, vanilla, and cinnamon; beat until combined well.
(cont.)

GLAZE:
2¼ teaspoons instant espresso powder
½ tablespoon boiling water
3 ounces fine-quality bittersweet (not sweetened) chocolate
1 tablespoon unsalted butter
¼ cup heavy cream

Dissolve espresso powder in boiling water. In double boiler or metal bowl set over saucepan of barely simmering water, combine chocolate and butter with cream and espresso mixture; melt ingredients over low heat, stirring until smooth. Remove top of double boiler or bowl from heat. Cool glaze to room temperature.

Cinnamon Toffee Bars

½ cup butter
2 cups brown sugar, packed
2 eggs, beaten
2 teaspoons vanilla
2 cups flour
2 teaspoons baking powder

¼ teaspoon salt
1 teaspoon cinnamon
1 cup pecans, chopped
2 cups (12 ounces) semisweet
   chocolate chips

Cook butter and brown sugar in saucepan over low heat until mixture comes to a boil. Remove from heat and let cool. Preheat oven to 350°. Grease 12 x 18-inch jelly roll pan. In medium bowl, stir together butter mixture, eggs, and vanilla. Sift together flour, baking powder, salt, and cinnamon; stir into egg mixture until well blended. Then stir in pecans. Spread batter into prepared jelly roll pan. Bake in preheated oven for 25 minutes. Remove from oven and immediately sprinkle chocolate chips over bars. Let stand for 5 minutes, then spread chocolate evenly over entire surface. Cut into squares.

Cranberry Crunch Squares

1 (16 ounce) can jellied cranberry sauce
2⅓ cups rolled oats
¾ cup flour
1⅝ cups brown sugar, packed
1 cup butter, melted

Spread cranberry sauce in bottom of greased 9 x 13-inch baking pan. Stir oats, flour, brown sugar, and butter until mixture resembles coarse crumbs. Sprinkle crumb mixture over cranberry sauce. Bake at 350° for 25 minutes. Cool and cut into squares.

This Christmas, give from your heart—whether it's of your money, your time, or your talents. When others witness your generous spirit, it will catch on. Kindness is contagious!

Cream Cheese Bars

If you like cheesecake, these are a dream!

CRUST:
½ cup butter, softened
1 golden yellow cake mix

Mix butter and cake mix until crumbly. Spread in buttered 9 x 13-inch baking pan.

TOPPING:
1 pound powdered sugar
2 eggs
1 (8 ounce) package cream cheese, softened

Cream powdered sugar, eggs, and cream cheese. Spread over cake mix crust.
Bake at 350° for 35 minutes. Watch carefully—these bars burn easily.

Double-Chocolate Mud Bars

BASE:

½ cup butter, softened
1 cup sugar
2 large eggs, separated

1½ cups flour
1 teaspoon baking powder
½ teaspoon salt

Beat together butter and sugar. Add egg yolks one at a time. In different bowl, mix together flour, baking powder, and salt. Fold flour mixture into butter mixture. Press combined ingredients into greased 9 x 13-inch baking pan. Pack down firmly.

FILLING:

1 cup walnuts, chopped
½ cup semisweet chocolate chips

1 cup miniature marshmallows
1 cup M&M's (optional)

Sprinkle walnuts, chocolate chips, marshmallows, and M&M's over base mixture in pan.

TOPPING:

2 egg whites

1 cup brown sugar, packed

Beat egg whites at high speed until stiff peaks form. Fold in brown sugar. Spread over top of pan. Bake at 350° for 35 minutes. Cool completely; cut into squares.

One-Bowl Bar Cookies

Pressed for time? This recipe doesn't take much time or cleanup.

1 applesauce-raisin cake mix	2 eggs
¾ cup quick-cooking oats	2 tablespoons vegetable oil
¼ cup wheat germ	½ cup raisins
½ cup light molasses	½ cup flaked coconut
¼ cup orange juice	

Combine cake mix, oats, and wheat germ. Add molasses, orange juice, eggs, and oil. Stir until well blended, then add raisins and coconut. Spread in greased jelly roll pan. Bake at 375° for 20 minutes or until lightly browned and pulled away from pan's edge. Cool. Glaze before cutting.

ORANGE GLAZE:

2 cups powdered sugar	¼ to ⅓ cup orange juice

Blend ingredients together until thin enough to pour but thick enough to spread.

Rhubarb Bars

RHUBARB MIXTURE:

3 cups cut rhubarb
1½ cups sugar
1 teaspoon vanilla

2 tablespoons cornstarch
¼ cup water

Combine rhubarb, sugar, vanilla, cornstarch, and water.
Cook over medium heat until thick.

CRUST:

1½ cup oats
1 cup brown sugar
1 cup shortening (part margarine)

½ cup walnuts, chopped
1½ cups flour
½ teaspoon baking soda

Combine all crust ingredients; pat three-quarters of crust mixture into 9 x 13-inch baking pan. Pour and spread cooked rhubarb mixture over crust. Sprinkle remaining crust mixture on top. Bake at 375° for 30 to 35 minutes.

Rocky Road Squares

BASE:

4 squares unsweetened chocolate   1 tablespoon milk
¾ cup butter   1 cup flour
1½ cups sugar   1 cup nuts, chopped
3 eggs

Heat chocolate and butter over low heat until butter melts; stir until smooth.
Stir in sugar. Mix in eggs and milk until well blended. Stir in flour and nuts.
Spread in greased 9 x 9-inch pan. Bake at 350° for 40 minutes. Add Rocky
Road Topping and bake for 10 minutes longer.

ROCKY ROAD TOPPING:

2 cups miniature marshmallows   1 cup nuts, chopped
1 cup semisweet chocolate chips

Layer ingredients over top of base.

Are your eggs fresh? To determine freshness, immerse the egg in a pan of cool, salted water. If it sinks, it is fresh, but if it floats on the surface, throw it out.

Seven-Layer Bars

½ cup butter
1 cup graham cracker crumbs
1 cup flaked coconut
1 cup (6 ounces) butterscotch chips
1 cup (6 ounces) semisweet chocolate chips
1 cup nuts, chopped
1 (14 ounce) can sweetened condensed milk

Preheat oven to 325°. Melt butter in 9 x 13-inch baking pan. Add next five ingredients in layers and carefully pour sweetened condensed milk on top.
Bake for 25 to 30 minutes or until slightly brown.

Strawberry Linzer Bars

1¾ cups flour
½ cup sugar
1 (2 ounce) package hazelnuts
    or blanched almonds,
    ground (½ cup)
1 teaspoon lemon zest
½ teaspoon cinnamon
½ teaspoon baking powder

¼ teaspoon salt
½ cup butter or margarine, cut up
1 egg, beaten
1 teaspoon vanilla
½ cup seedless strawberry or
    raspberry jam
Powdered sugar
Cinnamon

Mix flour, sugar, hazelnuts, lemon zest, cinnamon, baking powder, and salt. Add butter and beat at low speed until crumbly. Beat in egg and vanilla. Divide dough in half. Press half the dough into ungreased 9 x 9-inch pan. Spread jam on dough to within ½ inch of edge. Roll out other half of dough between two sheets of floured waxed paper, forming 10 x 11-inch rectangle. Remove waxed paper and cut dough into twenty ½-inch strips. Place strips over jam diagonally, forming lattice crust. Bake at 350° for 23 to 28 minutes. When cool, sprinkle with powdered sugar and cinnamon.
Store in refrigerator. Makes about 36 bars.

White Chocolate Squares

2 cups (12 ounces) white chocolate chips, divided
¼ cup butter or margarine
2 cups flour
½ teaspoon baking powder
1 teaspoon vanilla
1 (14 ounce) can sweetened condensed milk
1 cup pecans or walnuts, chopped
1 large egg
Powdered sugar

Preheat oven to 350°. Grease 9 x 13-inch baking pan. In large saucepan over low heat, melt 1 cup chips and butter. Stir in flour and baking powder until blended. Stir in vanilla, sweetened condensed milk, nuts, egg, and remaining chips. Spoon mixture into prepared pan. Bake for 20 to 25 minutes. Cool. Sprinkle with powdered sugar; cut into squares. Store covered at room temperature.

Festive Cakes & Pies

Time was with most of us, when Christmas Day, encircling all our limited world like a magic ring, left nothing out for us to miss or seek; bound together all our home enjoyments, affections, and hopes; grouped everything and everyone round the Christmas fire, and made the little picture shining in our bright young eyes complete.

CHARLES DICKENS

Almond Pound Cake

CAKE:

1 cup butter, softened
2 cups white sugar
6 eggs, room temperature
1¾ cups flour
½ teaspoon salt
2 teaspoons almond extract
½ cup blanched almonds

Preheat oven to 325°. Grease and flour 10-inch Bundt pan. In large bowl, cream butter and sugar until well mixed with electric mixer. Add eggs one at a time and beat until mixture is light and fluffy. Blend in flour and salt. Mix in almond extract. Turn batter into prepared pan. Bake for 60 minutes or until toothpick inserted in center of cake comes out clean. Cool in pan for 10 minutes. Remove from pan and transfer to a wire rack to continue cooling. When cake has cooled, drizzle with powdered sugar glaze. Top with blanched almonds and garnish with marzipan holly leaves and berries.

(cont.)

GLAZE:
1 cup powdered sugar
4 tablespoons milk

In small bowl, combine powdered sugar and milk. Mix until smooth.

GARNISH:
8 ounces almond paste
4 drops green food coloring
4 drops red food coloring

Break off tablespoon-sized pieces of almond paste and shape into holly leaves. Using knife tip, score shaped holly leaves to resemble veins in leaves. Mix green food coloring with small amount of water and brush holly leaves, repeating until desired color is reached. Set aside on waxed paper. Break off 2 tablespoons almond paste and knead in several drops of red food coloring. When paste is bright red, break off smaller pieces.
Roll into balls to resemble holly berries. Place on waxed paper.

Bûche de Noël
(Yule Log Cake)

1 cup flour	4 eggs
1¼ teaspoon baking powder	⅔ cup sugar
¼ teaspoon salt	1 tablespoon hot water
1 tablespoon cocoa	

Sift together flour, baking powder, salt, and cocoa. In bowl over pan of hot water, whisk together eggs and sugar until mixture is pale and thick. Remove from heat and fold in half the flour mixture. Fold in remaining flour mixture, along with hot water. Pour batter into lined jelly roll pan. Bake at 425° for about 10 minutes. Turn cake onto sheet of waxed paper and trim edges of cake. Before it cools, roll up cake with paper inside. Set aside to cool. When cool, unroll cake and remove paper. Spread one-quarter of filling on cake and roll it up. Spread rest of filling on outside of log. Use fork to make swirls and ridges like tree bark. Decorate with powdered sugar if desired.

FILLING:

½ cup butter or margarine, softened	2 tablespoons cocoa
2¼ cups powdered sugar	2 to 3 tablespoons milk

Mix butter and powdered sugar. Beat in cocoa and milk until mixture is fluffy.

Cherry Bundt Cake

1¼ cups butter, softened
2¾ cups sugar
5 eggs
1 teaspoon almond extract
3 cups flour
1 teaspoon baking powder

¼ teaspoon salt
1 cup unsweetened evaporated milk
1 cup maraschino cherries, well drained, quartered
Sifted powdered sugar

Beat butter, sugar, eggs, and extract in large bowl on low speed of electric mixer until blended, then on high speed for 5 minutes until light and fluffy. Combine flour, baking powder, and salt. To creamed mixture, alternately add dry ingredients and evaporated milk, mixing lightly after each addition. Fold in cherries. Turn batter into greased 12-cup Bundt or tube pan. Bake at 350° for 75 to 85 minutes. Cover with foil for last 10 minutes if becoming too brown. Cool in pan for 10 minutes, then remove from pan and cool completely. Dust with powdered sugar before serving.
A white icing drizzle is a pretty alternative garnish.

Create a personalized gift to give. Buy a fabric apron. Use fabric paint to write the recipient's name and to decorate the apron.

Classic Christmas Fruitcake

1 pound dark raisins
1 pound mixed fruit
3 pineapple rings
2 pounds sultana raisins
1 pound glazed cherries
1 pound mixed peel
1 pound blanched almonds
1 cup flour
2 cups butter, softened
1 pound sugar

12 eggs
2 ounces unsweetened chocolate, melted
1 cup grape jelly, softened
2½ cups flour
1 teaspoon baking soda
1 teaspoon salt
1 teaspoon nutmeg
1 teaspoon cloves
1 teaspoon allspice
2 tablespoons cinnamon

Pour boiling water on raisins and let sit for a few minutes. Drain and dry. Cover fruits, peel, and almonds with 1 cup flour. Mix well. Cream butter and sugar; add eggs one at a time and beat. Add melted chocolate and jelly. Sift together remaining flour, baking soda, salt, and spices. Add to fruit and mix well. Put two layers of brown paper (greased) in loaf tins and pour in batter. Bake at 275° for 4 to 5 hours. For smaller loaf pans, bake for only 2½ hours. Cool for 5 minutes and remove from pans.

Cranberry-Orange Coffee Cake

CRUMB TOPPING:
¾ cup flour
½ cup margarine, softened
½ cup sugar

Stir together flour, margarine, and sugar; set aside.

CREAM CHEESE LAYER:
1 (8 ounce) package cream cheese, softened
⅓ cup sugar
1 egg
1 teaspoon vanilla

Beat cream cheese and sugar until light and fluffy. Beat in egg and vanilla; set aside.

(cont.)

CAKE:

2 cups flour
1 cup sugar
1½ teaspoons baking powder
½ teaspoon baking soda
½ teaspoon salt
¾ cup orange juice

¼ cup margarine, softened
1 teaspoon vanilla
1 egg, beaten
2 cups fresh or frozen cranberries,
  coarsely chopped
2 tablespoons orange zest

Combine flour, sugar, baking powder, baking soda, and salt. Stir in juice, margarine, vanilla, and egg. Fold in cranberries and orange zest just until mixed. Pour into 9-inch springform pan. Spread cream cheese mixture over cake batter. Sprinkle with crumb topping. Bake at 350° for 65 to 70 minutes or until top springs back when lightly touched in center. Let cool on rack for 15 minutes. Remove outside ring of pan and let cool completely. Makes 12 servings.

Cream Cheese Apple Cake

PASTRY:

1¼ cups flour
⅓ cup sugar
½ cup margarine

1 egg yolk
¼ teaspoon vanilla

Mix flour with sugar. Cut in margarine. In separate bowl, beat egg yolk with vanilla. With fork, stir egg mixture into flour mixture. Press into bottom and halfway up sides of 9-inch springform pan.

TOPPING:

4 to 5 apples, peeled, cored, quartered, and scored
4 ounces cream cheese, softened
¾ cup sugar

1 teaspoon vanilla
2 eggs
½ cup light cream
Nutmeg to taste

Arrange apples on top of pastry. Beat cream cheese until fluffy. Gradually beat sugar and vanilla. Add eggs one at a time, then light cream. Pour topping over apples; sprinkle with nutmeg. Bake at 400° for 50 to 60 minutes. Serve warm or cool.

VARIATION: Use blueberries instead of apples.

Fruit Cocktail Cake

1 cup flour
1 cup sugar
1 teaspoon baking soda
½ teaspoon salt
1 egg, beaten
1 (15 ounce) can fruit cocktail, drained
½ cup brown sugar
½ cup flaked coconut

Mix flour, sugar, soda, and salt. Add egg and fruit cocktail. Pour into ungreased 8 x 8-inch pan. In separate bowl, mix brown sugar and coconut; spread over top of pan ingredients. Bake at 350° for 30 to 35 minutes.

Fudge Ribbon Cake

CHEESE MIXTURE:

2 tablespoons butter, softened
1 (8 ounce) package cream
   cheese, softened
¼ cup sugar
1 tablespoon cornstarch
1 egg

2 tablespoons sugar
1 tablespoon cornstarch
1 egg
2 tablespoons milk
½ teaspoon vanilla

CAKE MIXTURE:

2 cups flour
2 cups sugar
1 teaspoon salt
1 teaspoon baking powder
½ teaspoon baking soda
½ cup butter, softened

1 cup milk
⅓ cup milk
2 eggs
3 squares unsweetened chocolate,
   melted
1 teaspoon vanilla

(cont.)

Cream 2 tablespoons butter with cream cheese; add ¼ cup sugar and 1 tablespoon cornstarch. Add 1 egg, 2 tablespoons sugar, and 1 tablespoon cornstarch. Then add 1 egg, 2 tablespoons milk, and ½ teaspoon vanilla. Beat at high speed until smooth and creamy. Set aside. Grease and flour bottom of 13 x 9-inch baking pan. Combine flour with sugar, salt, baking powder, and baking soda in large mixing bowl. Add butter and 1 cup milk. Blend well at low speed. Add ⅓ cup milk, eggs, chocolate, and vanilla; continue beating 1½ minutes at low speed. Spread half of batter in pan. Spoon cheese mixture over batter. Top with remaining batter. Bake at 350° for 50 to 60 minutes. Cool and frost if desired.

Bake a cake and celebrate Christmas Eve with a birthday party for Jesus. Include the works—candles, ice cream, and balloons. Sing "Happy Birthday" to Jesus with your children. This is a great way to keep your focus on the true meaning of Christmas as well as establish a fun tradition for your family.

Gumdrop Cake

1 cup dates
1 cup raisins
1 cup butter
½ cup water
2 cups flour
2 eggs
1 teaspoon cinnamon

1 cup brown sugar
1 pound gumdrops, cut up
   (no black ones!)
1 cup sweetened applesauce
1 teaspoon baking soda
Nuts (optional)

Boil dates, raisins, butter, and water until raisins are tender. Let cool.
Add other ingredients. Bake at 350° for 1½ hours.

Honey Cake

1 cup brown sugar
5 eggs
1 cup creamed honey
1 cup vegetable oil
1 cup sour cream
2¾ to 3 cups flour
1¼ teaspoons baking powder
1¼ teaspoons baking soda

Beat sugar and eggs; add honey and beat well; add oil slowly, beating on lower speed until thoroughly blended. Add sour cream and beat. In separate bowl, combine flour, baking powder, and soda; add to batter. Beat slowly until smooth. Pour into greased 9 x 13-inch baking pan. Bake at 350° for approximately 1 hour.

Pineapple Dream Cake

36 large marshmallows
1 cup milk
1 pint whipping cream
1 cup crushed pineapple, drained
15 graham crackers

Melt marshmallows in milk over low heat; set aside. Whip cream, then fold pineapple into whipped cream; set aside. Crush graham crackers and cover bottom of 9 x 9-inch baking pan (save some for sprinkling). Add marshmallow mixture to pineapple mixture. Pour into pan. Sprinkle remaining crushed graham crackers on top. Chill before serving.

As you enter a friend's home or send your guests on to theirs, give a homemade gift of jam, drink mix, or baked goods.

Snickerdoodle Cake

1 German chocolate cake mix
1 (14 ounce) package caramels
½ cup margarine
⅓ cup milk
¾ cup semisweet chocolate chips
1 cup walnuts, chopped

Prepare cake mix, following package directions. Pour half of batter into greased
9 x 13-inch baking pan. Bake at 350° for 20 minutes. Melt caramels with margarine and
milk in saucepan over low heat, stirring frequently. Pour over baked cake. Sprinkle with
chocolate chips and nuts. Spoon remaining cake batter over caramel layer. Bake at 250°
for 20 minutes. Increase temperature to 350° and bake for an additional 10 minutes.

Sour Cream Chocolate Chip Cake

6 tablespoons butter, softened
1 cup sugar
2 eggs
1⅓ cups flour
1½ teaspoons baking powder
1 teaspoon baking soda
1 teaspoon cinnamon
1 cup sour cream
1 (6 ounce) package mini chocolate chips
1 tablespoon sugar

Mix butter and 1 cup sugar until blended. Beat in eggs one at a time. In separate bowl, combine flour, baking powder, soda, and cinnamon. Blend flour mixture with creamed mixture. Mix in sour cream. Pour batter into greased and floured 8 x 10-inch baking pan. Scatter chocolate chips evenly over batter. Then sprinkle 1 tablespoon sugar over top. Bake at 350° for 35 minutes or until cake just begins to pull away from sides of pan.

When preparing a cake pan, use a bit of the dry cake mix to flour the pan. This will soak into the cake and not leave a white mess.

Apple Cheesecake

BASE:

1 cup flour
½ cup butter, softened

½ cup sugar
¼ teaspoon vanilla

Mix ingredients until crumbly and press into bottom of greased 9-inch springform pan.

CREAM CHEESE MIXTURE:

2 (8 ounce) packages cream
cheese, softened
2 eggs

½ cup sugar
1 teaspoon vanilla

Beat ingredients and pour over base.

TOPPING:

4 cups tart apples, sliced
⅓ cup sugar

5 teaspoons cinnamon
¼ cup pecans or almonds, chopped

Shake apples in bag with sugar and cinnamon. Divide evenly on top of
cheesecake. Top with nuts. Bake at 325° for approximately 1 hour or
until center seems firm. Chill before serving.

Chocolate Chip Cheesecake

1½ cups chocolate sandwich cookie crumbs
3 tablespoons butter, melted
3 ounce packages cream cheese, softened
1 (14 ounce) can sweetened condensed milk
2 teaspoons vanilla
3 eggs
1 cup semisweet chocolate chips, divided
1 teaspoon flour

Combine cookie crumbs and butter; press into 9-inch springform pan. Beat cream cheese until fluffy, then beat in milk, vanilla, and eggs; set aside. In separate bowl, toss ½ cup chocolate chips with flour to coat; stir into cream cheese mixture. Pour batter into prepared pan; sprinkle with remaining chips. Bake at 300° for 1 hour or until cake springs back when lightly touched. Cool. Chill. Serve.

Magic Cherry Chiffon Cheesecake

1 9-inch piecrust (or 9-inch graham cracker crumb crust), unbaked
1 (3 ounce) package cream cheese, softened
7 ounces sweetened condensed milk
2 eggs, separated
2 tablespoons lemon juice
Pinch salt
1 can cherry pie filling

Bake piecrust according to package instructions. While crust is cooling, prepare filling. Beat cream cheese until fluffy. Add condensed milk and egg yolks; beat until smooth. Stir in lemon juice. In separate bowl, beat egg whites with salt until soft peaks form. Fold into mixture. Pour into baked piecrust. Bake at 300° for 30 minutes or until cake springs back when lightly touched. Chill and top with cherry pie filling.

VARIATION: Top with blueberry pie filling.

Pistachio Cheesecake

BASE:

½ cup butter or margarine, softened

3 tablespoons powdered sugar
1 cup flour

Mix together; press into 9 x 13-inch baking pan. Bake at 325° for 15 to 20 minutes; cool.

FILLING:

⅔ cup powdered sugar
⅔ large container frozen whipped topping, thawed

1 (8 ounce) package cream cheese, softened

Whip all filling ingredients; spread over cooled base.

TOPPING:

2 packages pistachio instant pudding

2½ cups milk

Whip above ingredients until slightly thick; pour over filling.
Top with remaining whipped topping and refrigerate.
VARIATION: Use chocolate instant pudding.

Pretzel Cheesecake

BASE:

1 cup pretzel crumbs   ½ cup sugar
¼ cup butter, melted

In 9-inch pie pan, combine pretzel crumbs, butter, and sugar.
Press into bottom of pan to form crust; set aside.

FILLING:

1 container frozen whipped   ½ cup powdered sugar
topping, thawed
1 (3 ounce) package cream
cheese, softened

Combine whipped topping, cream cheese, and powdered sugar in
medium bowl; beat well. Spread filling over prepared crust.

TOPPING:

1 (21 ounce) can cherry pie filling
Top cheesecake with cherry pie filling. Refrigerate for at least 2 hours before serving.

Want to do something inexpensive but heartfelt for your loved ones this Christmas? Send out Christmas cards that include a homemade coupon for one of your tasty desserts. Your friends and family will be delighted with this treat (and they'll be looking forward to what you have in store for them next Christmas!).

Any Fruit or Berry Pie

Fruit or berries, fresh or frozen (enough to fill piecrust)
¾ cup sugar
2 cups water
2 tablespoons cornstarch
Pinch salt
1 small package gelatin, same flavor as fruit
1 (9 inch) piecrust, baked and cooled
1 small container frozen whipped topping, thawed

Drain berries, pat dry, and sprinkle with sugar. Set aside. In saucepan, mix water, cornstarch, and salt. Bring to a boil; add gelatin and mix until dissolved. Continue to boil until syrupy. Remove from heat and let cool until right consistency to add fruit or berries. Gelatin mixture should be set enough to prevent fruit from sinking and cool enough to prevent fruit from cooking. Pour into piecrust. Chill completely. Top with whipped topping. Serve.

Banana Butterscotch Pie

2 cups milk
⅓ cup flour
¾ cup brown sugar
½ teaspoon salt
3 egg yolks, beaten
2 tablespoons butter
½ teaspoon vanilla
1 (9 inch) piecrust, baked and cooled
2 large bananas
Sweetened whipped cream

Heat milk slowly in double boiler or microwave. Add flour, brown sugar, and salt; cook until thick, stirring frequently with a whisk. Stir small amount into beaten egg yolks; return to main mixture and continue cooking 2 minutes longer. Remove from heat and beat in butter and vanilla. Cool slightly. Pour small amount over bottom of piecrust.
Slice one banana over top. Pour in remaining filling. Chill.
Garnish with one sliced banana and serve with whipped cream.

Christmas Angel Pie

1 (14 ounce) can sweetened condensed milk
⅓ cup lemon juice
1 (10 ounce) package frozen raspberries, thawed and drained
½ pint whipping cream, whipped
1 prepared graham cracker crumb or shortbread crust

Stir together sweetened condensed milk and lemon juice. Fold in raspberries
and whipped cream. Pour into prepared crust and chill.

Know someone who's lonely this holiday season? Remember them with a gift, a Christmas card, an invitation to your family's annual get-together, a ride to the Christmas Eve service. . .and share with them the love that Christ offers freely to all of us. Remind them that because of His love, we need never feel lonely, forgotten, or insignificant.

[Jesus said,] "Surely I am with you always."
MATTHEW 28:20

Cookies and Cream Pie

1 (3.9 ounce) package chocolate instant pudding
1 (8 ounce) container frozen whipped topping, thawed
1½ cups chocolate sandwich cookies, crushed
1 (9 inch) prepared chocolate crumb piecrust

Prepare pudding according to pie filling directions on package; allow to set. When pudding is set, fold in whipped topping. Add crushed cookies; stir. Pour mixture into prepared piecrust. Freeze pie until firm. Thaw in refrigerator before serving.

French Apple Pie (Torte)

BASE:

1⅓ cups flour

3 tablespoons powdered sugar

⅔ cup butter, softened

Combine flour and powdered sugar; cut in butter until crumbly.
Press dough in bottom and 2 inches up sides of 9-inch springform pan. Chill.

FILLING:

¾ cup sugar

¼ teaspoon salt

2 tablespoons flour

½ teaspoon cinnamon

2 tablespoons butter, softened

7 tart apples, thinly sliced

Combine sugar, salt, flour, and cinnamon; cut in butter. Add apples; toss to coat.
Spread filling mixture on top of base.

(cont.)

TOPPING:
1¼ cups flour
½ cup brown sugar, packed
⅓ cup butter, softened

Combine flour and brown sugar in bowl. Cut in butter. Squeeze handfuls of topping into firm chunks; break chunks apart into smaller pieces. Sprinkle over filling. Bake at 350° for 60 to 75 minutes or until apples are done. Cover loosely with foil if browning too quickly. Cool completely.

Grasshopper Pie

1 (8 ounce) package cream cheese, softened
1 (14 ounce) can sweetened condensed milk
Green food coloring
16 chocolate mint cookies, crushed
1 (8 ounce) container frozen whipped topping, thawed
1 (9 inch) prepared chocolate crumb piecrust

Place cream cheese in large bowl. Beat with electric mixer on low speed until fluffy.
Gradually beat in sweetened condensed milk until smooth. Add food coloring; stir.
Stir in crushed cookies, reserving some for garnish. Fold in reserving whipped topping.
Pour mixture into piecrust. Chill in refrigerator for 3 hours or until filling is set.
Garnish with remaining cookie pieces. Store in refrigerator.

Impossible Cherry Pie

CRUST:
1 cup milk
¼ teaspoon almond extract
½ cup all-purpose baking mix
2 tablespoons butter or margarine
2 eggs
¼ cup sugar

In blender, mix all crust ingredients for 15 seconds on high, or mix 1 minute on high speed with electric hand mixer. Pour into greased 10-inch pie plate.

FILLING:
1 (21 ounce) can cherry pie filling

Pour cherry pie filling into piecrust. Bake at 350° for 25 minutes.

(cont.)

STREUSEL TOPPING:
2 tablespoons butter or margarine
½ cup brown sugar
½ cup all-purpose baking mix
½ teaspoon cinnamon

While filled crust is baking, make topping by cutting butter into dry ingredients until mixture is crumbly. When pie comes out of oven, sprinkle with topping and return to oven until brown, about 10 minutes. Cool and serve. Store in refrigerator.

Peach Pie

CRUST:
1½ cups flour
½ cup margarine, softened
Pinch salt

Mix flour, margarine, and salt; press into an 8 x 8-inch baking pan.

FILLING:
1 (15 ounce) can peaches, halved
1 cup sugar
½ teaspoon cinnamon

Drain peaches, reserving ½ cup juice. Place peaches on top of crust.
Mix sugar and cinnamon and sprinkle over peaches.
Bake at 350° for 20 minutes. Remove from oven and let stand.

(cont.)

CUSTARD:
1 egg
½ cup peach juice
1 cup evaporated milk

Mix together egg, peach juice, and evaporated milk. Pour mixture on top of peaches and bake at 375° for an additional 30 minutes or until custard is set.

Pecan Pie

1 pastry shell, unbaked
1 cup pecans
3 eggs
½ cup sugar
1 cup light corn syrup
⅛ teaspoon salt
1 teaspoon vanilla
¼ cup butter, melted

Line pie plate with pastry. Spread pecans on top. Set aside. Beat eggs; add sugar, corn syrup, salt, vanilla, and melted butter. Pour over top of pecans.
Bake at 350° for 50 to 60 minutes.

Perfect Lemon Pie

FILLING:

7 tablespoons cornstarch

1½ cups sugar

½ teaspoon salt

2 cups boiling water

3 egg yolks

¼ cup lemon juice

2 tablespoons butter

2 tablespoons lemon zest

1 (9 inch) piecrust, baked

In saucepan, combine cornstarch, sugar, and salt. Add water. Cook until thick, stirring constantly. In separate bowl, beat egg yolks slightly. Add a little hot water mixture; stir and pour back into main mixture. Cook for 2 minutes, stirring constantly. Remove from heat and stir in lemon juice, butter, and lemon zest. Cool to room temperature without stirring. Pour into piecrust.

(cont.)

MERINGUE:
3 egg whites
6 tablespoons sugar
Pinch cream of tartar
Pinch salt

Beat egg whites until a fine foam mounds. Add sugar 1 tablespoon at a time. Beat after each addition; with last addition, add cream of tartar and salt. Beat until consistency is right. Spread over filling and bake at 350° for 15 minutes or until slightly golden.

When juicing a lemon, bring it to room temperature and roll it under your palm along the counter before cutting and squeezing. This action should release the most juice.

Pumpkin Ice Cream Pie

CRUST:

1½ cups gingersnap crumbs   ⅓ cup butter, melted
⅓ cup sugar

Combine gingersnap crumbs, sugar, and butter; mix well. Press into 9-inch pie plate.
Refrigerate until needed.

FILLING:

1 envelope unflavored gelatin   2¼ teaspoons pumpkin pie spice
¼ cup cold water   1½ teaspoons vanilla
¾ cup canned pumpkin   6 cups vanilla ice cream, softened
¾ teaspoon salt

In large saucepan, soften gelatin in cold water. Stir in pumpkin, salt, and pie spice. Stir
over low heat until gelatin is dissolved. Add vanilla and cool to room temperature. Fold
ice cream into mixture. Pour into prepared piecrust. If desired, sprinkle with additional
gingersnap crumbs. Freeze until firm. Remove from freezer 10 minutes before serving.

Pumpkin Pecan Pie

1 (15 ounce) can pumpkin
1 cup sugar
½ cup dark corn syrup
1 teaspoon vanilla
1 cup pecans, halved
½ teaspoon cinnamon
¼ teaspoon salt
3 eggs
1 (9 inch) piecrust, unbaked

Preheat oven to 350°. In large mixing bowl, blend together first seven ingredients. Add eggs and mix well. Pour into unbaked piecrust and top with additional pecans. Bake for 40 to 50 minutes or until knife inserted 1 inch from edge of pie comes out clean.

Christmassy Candies

For he himself is our peace.
EPHESIANS 2:14

Almond Roca

1 tablespoon light corn syrup
¼ cup sugar
1 cup butter
¼ cup water
1¼ cups toasted slivered almonds
1 cup semisweet chocolate chips

In large, heavy saucepan, gently boil syrup, sugar, butter, and water until mixture reaches "hard crack" stage on candy thermometer (300°F/150°C). Do not stir! This takes about 10 minutes. (To be certain mixture is ready, drop a small amount into cold water to see if it turns brittle.) Remove mixture from heat; add almonds. Spread onto ungreased cookie sheet. Sprinkle with chocolate chips while still hot; spread evenly when chips are melted. Cool in refrigerator or freezer. Break into bite-sized pieces.
Note: Do not double recipe.

Basic Buttercream Fondant
The following fondant recipe is used as the filling for chocolate-covered candy.

1 cup butter, softened
2 pounds powdered sugar
7 ounces marshmallow cream

Mix all ingredients together with hands, kneading until smooth. Makes about 2½ pounds of fondant. Coat candy molds with chocolate flavor of choice, then place small amount of fondant on chilled chocolate. Coat with chocolate to seal, then chill.

FLAVOR VARIATIONS:

CHOCOLATE CREAM:
⅓ recipe Buttercream Fondant
¼ cup cocoa

PEANUT BUTTER CREAM:
⅓ recipe Buttercream Fondant
¼ cup creamy peanut butter

PEPPERMINT CREAM:
⅓ recipe Buttercream Fondant
Peppermint flavoring to taste

MAPLE-NUT CREAM:
⅓ recipe Buttercream Fondant
Maple flavoring to taste
½ cup walnuts or pecans, finely chopped

CHERRY-NUT CREAM:
⅓ recipe Buttercream Fondant
¼ cup maraschino cherries, chopped
Cherry juice
¼ cup walnuts, chopped

Mix maraschino cherries, cherry juice for flavoring, and walnuts.
If recipe is too runny, add powdered sugar.

Brigadeiras

4 tablespoons butter or margarine
1 (14 ounce) can sweetened condensed milk
2 tablespoons cocoa
Sugar, chocolate, or colored sprinkles

Melt butter in saucepan. Add sweetened condensed milk and cocoa; cook over medium heat. Cook and stir constantly until very thick—about 5 or 10 minutes—until bottom of pan can easily be seen. Let cool. Roll into balls quickly.
Then roll in sugar, chocolate, or colored sprinkles. Makes 2 to 3 dozen candies.

Buckeyes

1 cup powdered sugar   3 tablespoons butter or margarine, softened
½ cup creamy peanut butter   1 pound milk chocolate

In large mixing bowl, stir together powdered sugar, peanut butter, and butter until well combined. Shape into about thirty 1-inch balls. Place balls on cookie sheet lined with waxed paper. Let stand for about 25 minutes or until dry. Place water in bottom of double boiler to within ½ inch of upper pan. Make sure upper pan does not touch water. While balls are cooling and water is heating, finely chop the chocolate so it will melt quickly. Bring water to a boil. Remove from heat and place about one-quarter of chocolate in top of double boiler. Stir until melted. Add about ½ cup more, stir, and repeat until all chocolate is melted. Stir until chocolate reaches 120°; reheat, if necessary, to reach this temperature. After chocolate has reached 120°, refill bottom of double boiler with cool water to within ½ inch of upper pan. Stir frequently until chocolate cools to 83°. This should take about 30 minutes. Using a toothpick, dip balls in chocolate, working quickly and stirring chocolate frequently to keep it evenly heated. Place balls on cookie sheet. (Chocolate will stay close to 83° for about 30 minutes. If temperature falls below 80°, chocolate must be remelted.) Store tightly covered in a cool, dry place. Makes about 30 pieces of candy.

Caramel Creams

3 cups sugar
1 cup light corn syrup
1 cup heavy whipping cream

In saucepan, combine all ingredients. Boil mixture gently for 10 to 15 minutes or until a small quantity dropped in cold water forms a firm ball. Beat until thick, then cool enough to handle. There are three options to shape/finish:

(1) Roll in small balls and dip in melted semisweet chocolate.
(2) Add 3 to 4 drops oil of peppermint to mixture, pour into pan, and cut in squares.
(3) Shape into cylinders about 1 inch in diameter, roll in chopped pecans, and slice.

Cherry Surprises

½ cup butter, softened
1¾ cups powdered sugar
1 teaspoon orange juice
1½ cups flaked coconut
1 (10 ounce) jar stemless maraschino cherries, drained

In medium bowl, combine butter, powdered sugar, and orange juice. Stir in coconut and mix until well combined. Wrap coconut mixture around each cherry to cover completely. Store in airtight container in refrigerator until ready to serve.

Chow Mein Candies

2 cups (12 ounces) semisweet chocolate chips
2 cups (12 ounces) butterscotch chips
2 (3 ounce) cans chow mein noodles
½ cup cashews

In large saucepan, combine chocolate chips and butterscotch chips. Melt over low heat, stirring constantly, until smooth. Remove from heat and stir in noodles and cashews. Drop by teaspoonfuls onto sheet of waxed paper and let cool until set. Store in airtight container.

Christmas Crunch

2 cups sugar
⅔ cup light corn syrup
½ cup water
3 tablespoons butter
1 teaspoon vanilla
½ teaspoon baking soda
2 cups crispy rice cereal
1 cup cashews

Grease 10 x 15-inch baking pan. In large saucepan over medium heat, combine sugar, corn syrup, and water; bring to a boil, stirring constantly until sugar is dissolved. Continue to cook, without stirring, until candy thermometer reads 300°. Remove from heat; stir in butter, vanilla, and baking soda. Add cereal and cashews; pour into prepared pan and allow to cool. Break into pieces and store in airtight container.

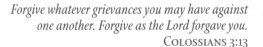

Holding on to an old grudge? Pray for the Lord to touch your heart and influence you with the spirit of forgiveness. Then give the gift of forgiving and forgetting. You'll be amazed at how much lighter your heart feels after this gesture of love and grace. (And your holiday will be merrier!)

Forgive whatever grievances you may have against one another. Forgive as the Lord forgave you.
COLOSSIANS 3:13

Christmas Turtle Candies

Vegetable oil spray
4 ounces pecans, halved
24 caramels
1 cup (6 ounces) semisweet chocolate chips
1 teaspoon shortening

Preheat oven to 300°. Cover cookie sheet with aluminum foil, shiny side up. Lightly grease foil with vegetable oil spray. Place three pecan halves in Y shape on foil. Place one caramel candy in center of each Y. Repeat. Bake just until caramel is melted, about 9 to 10 minutes. In saucepan, heat chocolate chips and shortening over low heat just until chocolate is melted. Spread over candies and refrigerate for 30 minutes. Makes 24 turtle candies.

Coconut Frogs

½ cup cocoa
2 cups sugar
½ cup milk
½ cup butter
1 teaspoon vanilla
1 cup flaked coconut
3 cups quick-cooking oats

Line two cookie sheets with waxed paper; set aside. In large saucepan, stir together cocoa, sugar, milk, and butter. Boil for 5 minutes; remove from heat. Stir in vanilla, coconut, and oats. Mix well. Drop by tablespoonfuls onto prepared cookie sheets. Refrigerate for 1 hour or until set. Store in refrigerator.

Cranberry Fudge

4 cups sugar
¼ cup unsalted butter
⅔ cup milk
1 tablespoon light corn syrup
1 (7 ounce) can full-cream condensed milk
¾ cup fresh cranberries

Mix sugar, butter, milk, and corn syrup in heavy saucepan and bring slowly to a boil, stirring constantly. Add condensed milk and return to a boil for 20 minutes, while continuing to stir, until mixture reaches 250° or when a small amount dropped into very cold water sets hard. Remove from heat and stir in cranberries. Spread in well-greased jelly roll pan and cut into squares just before fudge hardens. When completely cooled, cut into pieces and store in airtight container. Yields 2 pounds of candy.

Fantastic Fudge

⅔ cup evaporated milk
1⅔ cups sugar
1½ cups semisweet chocolate chips
1½ cups miniature marshmallows
½ teaspoon salt
1 teaspoon vanilla

In saucepan, combine milk and sugar; bring to a boil for 5 minutes.
Add chocolate chips and marshmallows. Stir until blended.
Add salt and vanilla and pour into buttered 8 x 8-inch baking dish to cool.

FLAVOR VARIATIONS:

MOCHA:
Dissolve 2 teaspoons instant coffee granules in 1 teaspoon hot water. Add with chocolate.

MINT:
Substitute ¾ cup mint chips and ¾ cup chocolate chips for chocolate chips.

MARBLE:
Substitute white chocolate chips for chocolate chips. After pouring fudge mixture into baking dish, drizzle with melted chocolate chip and swirl with knife for marble effect.

CHOCOLATE ORANGE:
Add 2 teaspoons freshly grated orange peel.

PEANUT BUTTER:
Substitute peanut butter chips for chocolate chips.

WHITE ALMOND:
Substitute white chocolate chips and ½ cup slivered almonds for chocolate chips.

MAPLE:
Substitute butterscotch chips and add maple flavoring to taste.

Festive Holiday Bark

16 ounces vanilla-flavored powdered coating
2 cups small pretzel twists
½ cup red and green candy-coated chocolate pieces

Line cookie sheet with waxed paper or parchment paper. Place powdered coating in microwave-safe bowl. Microwave for 2½ minutes. Stir; microwave at 30-second intervals until completely melted and smooth. Place pretzels and candy-coated chocolate pieces in large bowl. Pour melted coating over top and stir until well coated. Spread onto lined baking sheet. Let stand until firm or place in refrigerator to set up faster. Store in container at room temperature.

Five-Minute Never-Fail Fudge

⅔ cup evaporated milk
1⅓ cups sugar
¼ teaspoon salt
¼ cup butter
16 large marshmallows, cut up
1½ cups semisweet chocolate chips
1 teaspoon vanilla
1 cup walnuts, broken

In large saucepan, mix together milk, sugar, salt, butter, and marshmallows; bring to a boil, stirring constantly. Boil for 5 minutes. Remove from heat. Add chocolate chips and stir until melted. Stir in vanilla and walnuts. Spread in buttered 8 x 8-inch pan. Cool until firm.

Melt-in-Your-Mouth Toffee

2 cups butter or margarine
1 cup sugar
1 cup brown sugar, packed
1 cup walnuts, chopped
2 cups (12 ounces) semisweet chocolate chips

In heavy saucepan, combine butter and sugars. Cook over medium heat, stirring constantly until mixture boils. Boil to brittle stage—300°—without stirring. Remove from heat. Pour nuts and chocolate chips into 9 x 13-inch baking pan. Pour hot mixture over nuts and chocolate. Let mixture cool and break into pieces before serving.

Milk Chocolate Popcorn

12 cups popcorn, popped
2½ cups salted peanuts
1 cup light corn syrup
1 (11.5 ounce) package milk chocolate chips
¼ cup butter or margarine

Preheat oven to 300°. Grease large roasting pan. Line large bowl or serving plate with waxed paper. Combine popcorn and nuts in prepared roasting pan. Combine corn syrup, morsels, and butter in medium heavy-duty saucepan. Cook over medium heat, stirring constantly, until mixture boils. Pour over popcorn; toss well to coat. Bake, stirring frequently, for 30 to 40 minutes. Cool slightly in pan; transfer to prepared serving plate. Store in airtight container for up to two weeks.

Mocha Meringue Kisses

These candies are heart smart!

3 egg whites
¼ teaspoon cream of tartar
⅔ cup sugar, divided
½ teaspoon vanilla
2 teaspoons cornstarch
1 tablespoon instant coffee granules, crushed
¼ cup almonds, finely chopped

Beat egg whites with cream of tartar until frothy; gradually add ⅓ cup sugar and beat until stiff. Add vanilla. In separate bowl, mix ⅓ cup sugar with cornstarch, coffee powder, and nuts. Fold in egg white mixture. Spoon onto parchment-lined baking sheets. Bake in preheated 300° oven for 30 minutes. Turn off oven. Allow candies to cool in oven. Tops should be dry and slightly browned.

VARIATION: Use cocoa powder instead of instant coffee.

Peanut Butter Cups

2 to 3 pounds melting chocolate
1 cup graham cracker crumbs (7½ whole crackers, crushed)
1 cup butter, melted
¾ cup peanut butter
1 pound powdered sugar

Coat small paper cup liners with melted chocolate to cup edge; chill. Mix remaining
ingredients; add mixture to baking cups and cover with chocolate. Chill until firm.

Peanut Butter Fudge

2 cups sugar
½ cup milk
1½ cups peanut butter
1 (7 ounce) jar marshmallow cream

Butter baking pan (size depends on desired thickness of fudge). Set aside. In saucepan, bring sugar and milk to a boil. Boil for 3 minutes. Add peanut butter and marshmallow cream; mix well and fast. Quickly pour into prepared pan. Chill until set. Cut into squares.

Soft Peanut Butter Peanut Brittle

A softer alternative to a traditional holiday favorite.

2 cups sugar
¼ cup water
1½ cups light corn syrup
2 cups salted peanuts
2 to 2½ cups peanut butter
½ teaspoon vanilla
1½ teaspoons baking soda

Butter cookie sheet. Set aside. Combine sugar and water in heavy saucepan. Bring mixture to full rolling boil over high heat, stirring constantly. Stir in corn syrup. Cook to hard-crack stage—300°. Meanwhile, mix peanuts, peanut butter, and vanilla. Remove syrup from heat; at once add peanut butter mixture and baking soda; stir. Working quickly, pour onto prepared cookie sheet; spread with fork. Cool; break into pieces.

Dress up your dessert buffet with food shapes. Thread gum drops, cranberries, marshmallows, or popcorn onto a thin-gauge wire. Gently form into a simple shape such as a heart, circle, or star.

Sweet 'n' Simple
No-Bake Desserts

*Let us now go even unto Bethlehem, and see this thing which is come to pass,
which the Lord hath made known unto us.*

LUKE 2:15 KJV

Banana Split Pie

1 (3.9 ounce) package vanilla
  instant pudding

1¼ cups cold milk

1 (12 ounce) container frozen whipped
  topping, thawed and divided

2 bananas, sliced into ¼-inch slices,
  divided

1 (9 inch) prepared chocolate crumb
  crust

1 (12 ounce) jar hot fudge topping

1 (20 ounce) can pineapple chunks,
  drained

12 maraschino cherries with stems,
  drained

3 tablespoons walnut pieces

In large bowl, stir together pudding mix and milk. Beat until smooth and thick. Fold in 2 cups whipped topping and one sliced banana. Reserve one half the banana pudding mixture and spread remainder into piecrust. Reserve 3 tablespoons hot fudge topping for drizzling on top. Gently spread half of the remaining hot fudge topping over banana pudding in piecrust. Repeat layers with remaining banana pudding and fudge topping. Refrigerate for 1 hour or until firm. Arrange pineapple chunks in single layer on top of pie. Spread with remaining whipped topping, swirling topping into peaks with back of spoon. Refrigerate for 30 minutes. Heat reserved fudge topping in microwave until hot enough to pour. Using a fork, drizzle topping over pie. Garnish with maraschino cherries and walnut pieces.

Cheesecake Pudding

1 (8 ounce) package cream cheese, softened
½ cup butter, softened
1 cup powdered sugar
2 (3.9 ounce) packages vanilla instant pudding
3 cups milk
1 small container frozen whipped topping, thawed
3 cups chocolate sandwich cookie crumbs

In large bowl, mix cream cheese, butter, and powdered sugar until well blended. In separate bowl, combine pudding mixes and milk; mix well. Add whipped topping. Pour pudding mixture into cream cheese mixture and stir until completely blended. In parfait glasses, layer cookie crumbs and pudding mixture, ending with the cookie crumbs. Continue filling glasses until mixture is gone.

Cherry Christmas Dessert

1 (21 ounce) can cherry pie filling
1 (8 ounce) container frozen whipped topping, thawed
1 (14 ounce) can sweetened condensed milk
1 (10 ounce) can crushed pineapple, drained
1 package cherry gelatin
½ cup nuts, chopped

Combine all ingredients in large bowl; mix well.
Refrigerate for at least 4 hours before serving.

Christmas Dessert Pudding

4 (14 ounce) cans sweetened condensed milk
4 pints heavy whipping cream
1 (4 ounce) jar stemless maraschino cherries, drained
1 cup almonds, chopped

Remove labels from cans of sweetened condensed milk and put unopened cans into large pot of gently boiling water. Boil for about 3 hours, making sure water doesn't boil away. After 3 hours, take cans out and chill in refrigerator. When chilled, open cans and pour contents into large bowl. In medium bowl, beat whipping cream until thick; fold into bowl of sweetened condensed milk. Stir in cherries and almonds.

Christmas Orange Balls

4 cups graham cracker crumbs
1 cup powdered sugar
1 cup pecans, chopped
¼ cup light corn syrup
1 (6 ounce) can frozen orange juice concentrate, thawed
¼ cup butter, melted
⅓ cup powdered sugar

In medium bowl, stir together graham cracker crumbs, 1 cup powdered sugar, and pecans. Make a well in center of mixture and pour in corn syrup, orange juice concentrate, and melted butter. Mix well by hand until dough forms. Roll into 1-inch balls and roll balls in powdered sugar. Store at room temperature in an airtight container with sheet of waxed paper between layers to prevent sticking.

Coffee Chocolate Dessert

Graham cracker squares (not crumbs)
2 cups whipping cream
½ cup powdered sugar
4 tablespoons chocolate syrup
1 tablespoon instant coffee granules
Chocolate garnish (shaved chocolate or chocolate sprinkles)

Place layer of graham crackers in 9 x 9-inch pan. Whip cream; add powdered sugar, chocolate topping, and instant coffee. Mix well. Spread one-third of whipped cream mixture on crackers. Top with another layer of crackers, then add second third of mixture; top with crackers and last third of mixture. Sprinkle with chocolate garnish.

Surprise one of the neighborhood families with a tasty dessert from your kitchen. Attach a note that reads "This Christmas, I wish you hope." And include a scripture passage or quotation with a holiday message or theme. Martha and I suggest the following:

This is Christmas: not the tinsel, not the giving and receiving, not even the carols, but the humble heart that receives anew the wondrous gift, the Christ.
FRANK McKIBBEN

And she shall bring forth a son, and thou shalt call his name JESUS: for he shall save his people from their sins.
MATTHEW 1:21 KJV

Cranberry Storm

1 cup graham cracker crumbs
¼ cup butter, melted
1 small package cranberry gelatin
⅔ cup boiling water
1 cup cold water
½ cup whole cranberry sauce
Zest of 1 orange
1 orange, peeled and sectioned
1 (8 ounce) container frozen whipped topping, thawed

Mix crumbs and butter and press into 9 x 9-inch baking pan; set aside. Mix gelatin with ⅔ cup boiling water, then 1 cup cold water. Stir in cranberry sauce, orange zest, and orange sections. Fold in whipped topping. Chill until slightly thickened, about 10 minutes. Spoon into crust. Freezes well.

No-Bake Chocolate Dessert

20 chocolate sandwich cookies, crushed
1 (8 ounce) package cream cheese, softened
2 cups powdered sugar
¾ cup peanut butter
1 (12 ounce) container frozen whipped topping, thawed

Press crushed cookies into bottom of 9 x 13-inch baking pan, reserving some for garnish. In medium bowl, combine cream cheese and powdered sugar; beat well. Stir in peanut butter until well blended. Fold in whipped topping. Spread mixture over crushed cookie layer. Sprinkle reserved crushed cookies over top. Freeze for 1 to 2 hours. Thaw for 10 to 15 minutes before cutting and serving.

No-Bake Fruitcake

1 cup pecans, chopped
1 cup raisins, chopped
1 cup walnuts, chopped
1 (4 ounce) jar stemless maraschino cherries, drained and chopped
1 (14 ounce) can sweetened condensed milk
1 (12 ounce) package vanilla wafers, crushed

In medium bowl, combine pecans, raisins, walnuts, cherries, sweetened condensed milk, and vanilla wafers. Dough will be thick; use hands to mix completely. Shape dough into ring on dinner plate. Wrap cake and plate in many layers of plastic wrap. Refrigerate cake for at least one week to allow flavors to blend and all of milk to be absorbed.

No-Bake Peanut Chocolate Brownies

4 cups graham cracker crumbs
1 cup peanuts, chopped
½ cup powdered sugar
¼ cup peanut butter
2 cups (12 ounces) semisweet chocolate chips
1 cup evaporated milk
1 teaspoon vanilla

Grease 9 x 9-inch pan; set aside. In medium bowl, combine graham cracker crumbs, peanuts, powdered sugar, and peanut butter with pastry blender. In small saucepan over low heat, melt chocolate chips with evaporated milk, stirring constantly. Remove from heat and stir in vanilla. Remove ½ cup melted chocolate mixture and set aside. Pour remaining chocolate mixture over graham cracker crumb mixture and stir until well blended. Spread evenly in prepared pan. Frost with reserved chocolate mixture. Chill in refrigerator for at least 1 hour.

No-Bake Pumpkin Pie

4 ounces cream cheese, softened
1 tablespoon milk
1 tablespoon sugar
1½ cups frozen whipped topping, thawed
1 (9 inch) prepared graham cracker crust
1 cup cold milk
2 (3.9 ounce) packages vanilla instant pudding
1 (15 ounce) can pumpkin puree
1 teaspoon ground cinnamon
½ teaspoon ground ginger
¼ teaspoon ground cloves
Additional frozen whipped topping, thawed

In large bowl, whisk together cream cheese, milk, and sugar until mixture is smooth. Fold in 1½ cups whipped topping; stir well. Spread mixture onto bottom of prepared crust. In large bowl, combine milk, pudding mixes, pumpkin, cinnamon, ginger, and cloves; mix well. When pudding mixture is thick, spread it over cream cheese layer. Refrigerate for 4 hours or until set. Garnish with whipped topping. Keep refrigerated.

Oatmeal Macaroons

½ cup shortening
½ cup milk
2 cups sugar
½ cup cocoa
½ cup flaked coconut
3 cups oats

In medium saucepan over medium heat, combine shortening, milk, and sugar. Bring mixture to a boil, stirring constantly. Boil for 2 minutes. Remove from heat and stir in cocoa, coconut, and oats; mix well. Drop mixture by spoonfuls onto waxed paper. Allow to cool for 2 to 3 hours. Store in airtight container.

Peanut Butter No-Bake Cookies

2 cups sugar
¾ cup butter
¾ cup milk
½ teaspoon vanilla
1½ cups peanut butter
4½ cups quick-cooking oats

In a medium saucepan, over medium heat, combine sugar, butter, and milk. Bring to a rolling boil and boil for 1 full minute. Remove from heat and stir in vanilla and peanut butter. Mix in oats and stir until mixture begins to cool.

Drop mixture by spoonfuls onto sheet of waxed paper. Allow to cool until set.

Pumpkin Parfait

1 can pumpkin puree
1 (3.9 ounce) package vanilla instant pudding
1 teaspoon pumpkin pie spice
1 cup evaporated milk
1 cup milk
Whipped topping (optional)

In large mixing bowl, combine pumpkin puree, pudding mix, pumpkin pie spice, evaporated milk, and milk. Stir until smooth. Place mixture in parfait glasses and chill until set. Top parfaits with whipped topping if desired.

Snowballs

1½ cups powdered sugar
2¼ cups chocolate sandwich cookie crumbs
1 cup pecans, finely chopped
⅓ cup flaked coconut
¼ cup light corn syrup
¼ cup strawberry preserves

Sift powdered sugar; set aside 1¼ cups. In large bowl, combine cookie crumbs, pecans, ¼ cup powdered sugar, and coconut; mix well. Stir in corn syrup and preserves.
Shape mixture into 1-inch balls.
Roll each ball in remaining powdered sugar. Store in airtight container.

Traditional No-Bake Cookies

½ cup butter or margarine
½ cup milk
2 cups sugar
½ cup cocoa
1 cup peanut butter
1 teaspoon vanilla
3 cups oats

Combine butter, milk, sugar, and cocoa in large saucepan. Bring to a rolling boil. Boil for 3 minutes (do not overboil); remove from heat, then add peanut butter, vanilla, and oats. Drop by heaping teaspoonfuls onto sheet of waxed paper. Let cool until firm. Store in airtight container in cool, dry place.

Miscellaneous Merry Desserts

May you have the gladness of Christmas, which is Hope.
AVA V. HENDRICKS

Black Forest Trifle

1 fudge cake mix
1 (5.9 ounce) package chocolate instant pudding
1 quart cherry pie filling
¾ quart whipped topping
Chocolate curls
Maraschino cherries

Prepare and bake fudge cake in two layers, then slice into chunks. Prepare chocolate pudding. In large bowl, layer chunks of chocolate cake, pudding, pie filling, and whipped topping—making three repetitions and ending with layer of cake and cream. Garnish with whipping cream, chocolate curls, and cherries. Chill and serve.

Bake a Christmas tree. Slice thin rounds from a log of refrigerated cookie dough. On a cookie sheet lined with parchment paper, start at one end, centering one slice. In the next row place two slices barely touching. Continue down the pan, enlarging your rows. Allow for a couple of slices of dough at the end to serve as the tree trunk. Bake for nearly double the time instructed on the dough package. The cooled tree can be decorated with icing and small candies.

Bread Pudding

PUDDING:

4 cups milk
3 cups bread, cubed
3 eggs, beaten
½ cup sugar

¼ teaspoon salt
1 teaspoon vanilla
2 tablespoons butter, melted

Scald milk. In large bowl, pour milk over bread cubes and let stand for 10 minutes. In separate bowl, beat eggs; then beat in sugar, salt, and vanilla. Pour over milk and bread. Drizzle melted butter over top and stir to combine. Pour into buttered baking dish. Bake at 350° for 1½ hours or until set. Serve with custard sauce.

CUSTARD SAUCE:

1 cup milk
2 tablespoons sugar
Dash salt

⅛ teaspoon cinnamon
2 egg yolks, beaten

Bring milk to a boil. In small bowl, beat sugar, salt, and cinnamon into egg yolks. Whisk egg mixture into boiling milk. Remove from heat. Chill before serving over bread pudding.

Cheese Blintzes

1 (1 pound) loaf white bread
¼ cup sugar
2 teaspoons cinnamon
2 (8 ounce) packages cream cheese, softened
2 egg yolks
½ cup sugar
1 teaspoon vanilla
½ cup butter, melted

Preheat oven to 350°. Trim crusts from bread and roll each slice flat. In small bowl, combine ¼ cup sugar and cinnamon. Set aside. In large mixing bowl, beat cream cheese, egg yolks, ½ cup sugar, and vanilla until smooth. Spread this mixture onto each slice of flattened bread. Roll bread slices up. Dip each roll in melted butter, then roll immediately in cinnamon-sugar mixture. Cut rolls into 1-inch pieces. Arrange blintzes on greased cookie sheet. Bake for 10 minutes.

Dear Heavenly Father, please touch the hearts of those who have no hope this holiday season. May all of those who are hurting and feeling there's no relief in sight experience Your Light in an unexpected way. Show them that through You—no matter how difficult their situation—there's always hope.

Chocolate Rainbow Rolls

½ cup butter or margarine
2 cups (12 ounces) semisweet chocolate chips
6 cups (10.5 ounces) miniature colored marshmallows
1 cup nuts, finely chopped
Additional chopped nuts

In medium saucepan over low heat, melt butter and chocolate chips until blended, stirring constantly. Remove from heat and cool for 5 minutes. Stir in marshmallows and 1 cup nuts. Do not let marshmallows melt. On sheet of waxed paper, shape mixture into two 7-inch rolls. Wrap rolls in aluminum foil and refrigerate for about 20 to 25 minutes. To coat rolls, roll them in additional nuts. Wrap and refrigerate overnight. Cut rolls into ¼-inch slices. Store in airtight container in cool, dry place. Makes about 3 dozen slices.

Christmas Bread

1 loaf frozen white bread dough, thawed
½ cup mixed candied fruit
¼ cup almonds, chopped or sliced
Butter or margarine, melted
2 tablespoons sugar
½ teaspoon cinnamon
Vanilla icing (optional)
Candied fruit
Slivered almonds

Let dough rise until doubled in size. Roll out on floured surface into 7 x 14-inch rectangle. Sprinkle half with fruit and almonds. Fold uncovered dough over fruits; roll out again. Shape into round ball. Place greased 9-inch round pan. Brush top with butter. Combine sugar and cinnamon. Sprinkle cinnamon-sugar mixture over top of loaf. Cover; let rise in warm place until doubled in size, about 1 to 1½ hours. Bake at 350° until golden brown, about 30 to 35 minutes. If desired, frost with vanilla icing and garnish with additional candied fruit and slivered almonds.

Christmas Shortbread

1 cup butter, softened
¼ cup sugar
2 cups flour
1½ cups flaked coconut
⅔ cup red or green cherries
¼ cup raisins or currants
⅓ cup walnuts or almonds, chopped
1 cup sweetened condensed milk (not evaporated)
Powdered sugar

Cream butter and sugar. Blend in flour until mixture resembles coarse crumbs. Pat into greased 9 x 9-inch pan. Bake at 350° for 20 minutes. Combine coconut, cherries, raisins, walnuts, and milk. Spread over shortbread and bake an additional 35 minutes or until golden brown. Cool and cut into bars. Dust with powdered sugar.

Christmas Wreaths

½ cup butter
30 large marshmallows
1½ teaspoons green food coloring
1 teaspoon vanilla
4 cups cornflakes cereal
2 tablespoons cinnamon candies

Melt butter in large saucepan over low heat. Add marshmallows and heat until completely melted, stirring constantly. Remove from heat and add food coloring, vanilla, and cornflakes. With lightly greased fingers, quickly drop spoonfuls of mixture onto waxed paper and form into wreath shapes. Immediately decorate with cinnamon candies. Cool at room temperature before removing from waxed paper. Store in airtight container.

Cocoa Krispie Roll

¾ cup light corn syrup
¾ cup sugar
¾ cup peanut butter
2 tablespoons butter
4½ cups crispy rice cereal
⅓ cup butter
2 tablespoons milk
1½ cups powdered sugar
⅔ cup cocoa

Cook corn syrup and sugar until sugar dissolves and mixture bubbles. Remove from heat; blend in peanut butter and 2 tablespoons butter. Add cereal; stir until well coated. Press firmly into buttered 10 x 15-inch jelly roll pan or cookie sheet. Melt ⅓ cup butter with milk over low heat. Remove from heat; sift in powdered sugar and cocoa. Blend thoroughly. Remove cereal from pan and place on waxed paper; spread evenly with cocoa mix. Starting at short end, roll up to form a log. Wrap in greased waxed paper; refrigerate until firm. Remove from refrigerator 30 minutes before serving. Cut into ½-inch slices.

Cranberry-Apricot Tartlets

TARTLET SHELLS:

¼ cup sugar
½ cup butter or margarine,
   cut into 4 pieces
1⅓ cups flour

¼ teaspoon salt
½ teaspoon orange zest
1 to 3 tablespoons orange juice

Combine sugar, butter, flour, and salt, beating at low speed until crumbly. Add orange zest and enough orange juice to form a dough. Divide dough into 30 equal pieces. Press dough in bottom and up sides of greased and sugared mini-muffin pan cups. Bake at 375° for 14 to 18 minutes. Loosen edges with knife and remove shells.

FILLING:

1½ cups fresh or frozen
   cranberries
¾ cup dried apricots, chopped
1 cup sugar

⅓ cup orange juice
¼ cup water
½ teaspoon orange zest
Sweetened whipped cream (optional)

Combine all filling ingredients except whipped cream, cooking over medium-high heat until mixture comes to a full boil. Stir occasionally. Reduce heat to low and cook for 15 to 20 minutes, stirring occasionally, until mixture is thickened. When filling is completely cooled, just before serving, spoon into shells. If desired, top with whipped cream. Makes 30 tartlets.

Cranberry-Orange Nut Bread

2 cups flour
¾ cup sugar
1½ teaspoons baking powder
¾ teaspoon salt
½ teaspoon baking soda
¼ cup margarine or butter, softened
1 tablespoon orange zest
¾ cup orange juice
1 egg
1 cup cranberries, chopped
½ cup nuts, chopped

Heat oven to 350°. Grease bottom only of 9 x 5 x 3-inch loaf pan. Combine flour, sugar, baking powder, salt, and baking soda; cut in margarine until crumbly. Add orange zest, orange juice, and egg; stir just until moistened. Mix in cranberries and nuts. Pour into prepared pan and bake for 55 to 65 minutes or until wooden toothpick inserted in center comes out clean. Cool completely before slicing.

Frozen Peanut Butter Mousse

1 egg white
¼ cup sugar
1 cup heavy cream
½ cup creamy peanut butter
½ cup milk
¼ cup light corn syrup
Dash salt
1 can whipped cream
4 maraschino cherries with stems

Beat egg white into soft peaks, then add sugar and beat into stiff peaks. Set aside. Beat cream until stiff; set aside. Beat peanut butter and milk until smooth. Mix in corn syrup and salt until well blended. Fold egg white mixture and cream mixture into peanut butter mixture until smooth and well blended. Pour into eight 4-ounce serving cups or one 1-quart bowl. Cover and freeze until firm, about 1 hour for small cups, 3 hours for single container. To serve, remove from freezer and let stand in fridge for 10 minutes (30 minutes for single container). Garnish with whipped cream and maraschino cherries.

Lemon Tarts

½ cup butter
2 cups sugar
2 lemons, zest and juice
4 eggs
24 mini tart shells, baked

Melt butter and sugar in double boiler. Add zest, then beat in eggs and lemon juice.
Boil to thicken. Spoon into baked tart shells. Cool.

Peanut Butter Logs

1 cup peanut butter
2 cups powdered sugar
1 cup walnuts, chopped
1 cup dates, chopped
4 squares semisweet chocolate, melted
Flaked coconut

Combine peanut butter, powdered sugar, walnuts, and dates. Mix like a pastry and roll dough into a small log. Dip or roll in chocolate, then roll in coconut.
If dough is too stiff to roll, add a little coffee or milk.

Peppermint Pudding

1 pint whipping cream
1 teaspoon vanilla
1 large red-and-white-striped candy cane, crushed
1 (10 ounce) package mini marshmallows
Vanilla wafers

Whip whipping cream and vanilla until stiff. Stir in crushed peppermint and marshmallows. Line clear glass dessert dish with vanilla wafers. Pour pudding into lined bowl. Chill for 3 to 4 hours—best if chilled overnight.

Popcorn Balls

½ cup sugar
½ cup light corn syrup
½ cup margarine or butter
½ teaspoon salt
Few drops food coloring
8 cups popcorn, popped

Simmer sugar, corn syrup, margarine, salt, and food coloring in 4-quart Dutch oven over medium-high heat, stirring constantly. Add popped corn and cook about 3 minutes, stirring constantly until popcorn is well coated. Cool slightly. After dipping hands into cold water, shape mixture into 2½-inch balls. Place on waxed paper; when cooled, wrap individually in plastic wrap. Makes 8 or 9 popcorn balls.

Puppy Chow

9 cups rice squares cereal
¼ cup butter or margarine
1 cup (6 ounces) semisweet chocolate chips
½ cup peanut butter
1 teaspoon vanilla
1½ cups powdered sugar, divided

Pour cereal into large bowl; set aside. In small microwave-safe bowl, combine butter, chocolate chips, and peanut butter. Microwave on high for 1 to 2 minutes or until chips are completely melted and smooth when stirred. Stir in vanilla. Pour mixture over cereal. Pour ¾ cup powdered sugar into large sealable plastic bag. Add half of cereal mixture to bag and seal top completely. Shake until cereal is evenly coated with powdered sugar. Pour cereal onto sheet of waxed paper. Pour remaining powdered sugar into bag, along with remaining cereal mixture. Seal opening and shake until coated. Pour onto waxed paper and cool completely. Store in airtight container in cool, dry place.

Rice Pudding

1 teaspoon butter
1 quart milk
1 cup white rice, cooked
½ cup sugar
¼ teaspoon salt
1 teaspoon cinnamon
2 eggs, beaten
1 teaspoon vanilla
½ cup raisins

Preheat oven to 350°. Butter 2-quart baking dish. In heavy saucepan over medium heat, scald milk; remove from heat. Stir in rice, sugar, salt, and cinnamon. Mix well; slowly add eggs and vanilla. Stir in raisins. Pour mixture into prepared baking dish.
Bake for 40 minutes, stirring halfway through cooking time.

S'more Mix

2 cups honey or cinnamon graham cereal
1 cup salted peanuts
1 cup miniature marshmallows
½ cup milk chocolate chips
½ cup raisins

Combine all ingredients in large, festive bowl. Makes 5 cups.

Give a gift of hope: Take some money normally reserved for your Christmas shopping and donate it to a charity that helps children who might not otherwise have a Christmas celebration.

Vanilla Party Mix

1 (10 ounce) package miniature pretzels
5 cups rice squares cereal
1 (1 pound) package candy-coated chocolate pieces
2 (12 ounce) packages vanilla chips
3 tablespoons vegetable oil

In large bowl, combine pretzels, cereal, and chocolate pieces; set aside. In small microwave-safe bowl, combine chips and vegetable oil. Microwave on high for 2 minutes. Stir and microwave on high for 10 more seconds. Stir until smooth. Pour over cereal mixture and mix well. Spread onto waxed paper and cool completely. Store in airtight container in cool, dry place.

Index

Also Available from Mary & Martha. . .

 *In the Kitchen with Mary & Martha*
ISBN 1-59310-878-8

 *One-Dish Wonders*
ISBN 1-59789-011-1

 *Cookin' Up Christmas*
ISBN 1-59789-239-4

224 pages • hardback with printed comb binding

Available Wherever Books Are Sold